D0641241

A Special Gift

For: _____

From: _____

Date: _____

Illustration Copyright ©1999 Judy Buswell
Text Copyright ©1999

The Brownlow Corporation
6309 Airport Freeway
Fort Worth, Texas 76117

Grateful appreciation is expressed to
Lara Lleverino for her research assistance

ISBN: 1-57051-171-3

Manufactured in China

Sisters

Compiled and Written by Caroline Brownlow

Illustrated *Judy Buswell*

Brownlow

LITTLE TREASURES
MINIATURE BOOKS

Grandmother

Grandmothers Are for Loving

Happiness Is Homemade

Mom, I Love You ❧ *My Sister, My Friend*

Quiet Moments of Inspiration

Quilted Hearts ❧ *Rose Petals*

Seasons of Friendship

Sisters

Soft As the Voice of an Angel

Tea Time Friends ❧ *They Call It Golf*

BEST FRIENDS ARE WE

We laugh— we cry—
We make time fly!
Best friends are we—
My sister and me!

I have a simple philosophy. Fill what's empty. Empty what's full. Scratch where it itches.

ALICE ROOSEVELT LONGWORTH

If we are ever going to have perfect love in our hearts, we must have the very nature of God in us.

OSWALD CHAMBERS

I wash everything on the gentle cycle.
It is much kinder and more humane.

We find rest in those we love,
and we provide a resting place
in ourselves for those who love us.

BERNARD OF CLAIRVAUX

How very good and pleasant it is when sisters
live together in unity, harmony and love.

PSALM 133:1 PARAPHRASE

There can be no situation in life
in which the conversation of my dear sister
will not administer some comfort to me.

LADY MARY WORTLEY MONTAGU

JUST LIKE HER SISTER

One thing in the shop I never learned to do as well as Betsie, and that was to care about each person who stepped through the door. Often when a customer entered I would slip out the rear door and up to Betsie in the kitchen. "Betsie! Who is the woman with the Alpine lapel-watch on a blue velvet band—stout, around fifty?"

"That's Mrs. van den Keukel. Her brother

came back from Indonesia with malaria and she's been nursing him, Corrie." As I sped back down the stairs, "Ask her how Mrs. Rinker's baby is!"

And Mrs. van den Keukel, leaving the shop a few minutes later, would comment mistakenly to her husband, "That Corrie ten Boom is just like her sister!"

CORRIE TEN BOOM

People from a planet without flowers
would think we must be mad
with joy the whole time
to have such things about us.

IRIS MURDOCH

He has made everything
beautiful in its time.

ECCLESIASTES 3:11

SISTERHOOD

There is space within sisterhood
for likeness and difference, for the
subtle differences that challenge
and delight; there is space for
disappointment—and surprise.

CHRISTINE DOWNING

Of all the people, [my sister's] stamp
of approval was most important because
she knew me better than anyone.

ANN KIEMEL

God sends no one away
empty except those who are
full of themselves

DWIGHT L. MOODY

Call it a clan, call it a network,
call it a tribe, call it a family. Whatever
you call it, whoever you are, you need one.

JANE HOWARD

The deepest truth blooms only
from the deepest love.

HEINRICH HEINE

Sisters, if they be true to the name,

have no solitary joys or sorrows.

Sisters cannot help but share them all.

ANONYMOUS

Few delights can equal the mere presence

of one whom we trust utterly.

GEORGE MACDONALD

There's nothing wrong with teenagers
that reasoning with them won't aggravate.

ANONYMOUS

I thank my God every time
I remember you. In all my prayers for you,
I always pray with joy.

PHILIPPIANS 1:3, 4

Keeping peace in the family

requires patience, love, understanding—

and at least two television sets.

ANONYMOUS

The family—that dear octopus from whose

tentacles we never quite escape, nor in our

inmost hearts, ever quite wish to.

DODIE SMITH

EVERYTHING IN LOVE

We shall one day forget all about duty,
and do everything from the love
of the loveliness of it, the satisfaction
of the rightness of it.

GEORGE MACDONALD

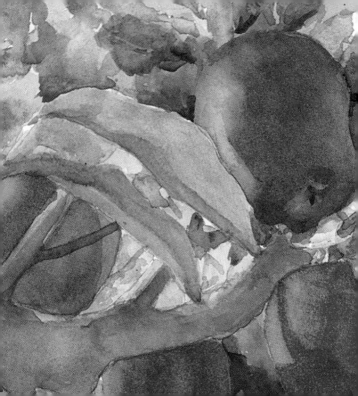

You know full as well as I do
the value of sisters' affections to each other;
there is nothing like it in this world.

CHARLOTTE BRONTË

"Consider the lilies," said the Master.
Truly, there is no more prayerful business
than this "consideration" of all
the flowers that grow.

CELIA THAXTER

Remember, we all stumble,
every one of us. That's why
it's a comfort to go hand in hand.

EMILY KIMBROUGH

One of life's major mistakes
is being the last member of the family
to get the flu—after all
the sympathy has run out.

ANONYMOUS

THE BLESSING

Having someplace
to go is home.

Having someone
to love is family.

Having both is a blessing.

If we laugh a lot, when we get older our wrinkles will all be in the right places.

ANONYMOUS

Love must be sincere. Hate what is evil; cling to what is good. Be devoted to one another in sisterly love. Honor one another above yourselves.

ROMANS 12:9, 10 PARAPHRASE

YOU ALWAYS KNOW

A sister always knows when to
listen and when to talk,
when to laugh and when to cry.

ANONYMOUS

THE BEST IN US

So much of what is best in us
is bound up in our love of family,
that it remains the measure of our
stability because it measures our
sense of loyalty. All other pacts
of love or fear derive from it
and are modeled upon it.

HANIEL LONG

If God took time to create beauty,
how can we be too busy to appreciate it?

RANDALL B. CORBIN

Enjoy the little things for one day
you may look back and realize
they were the big things.

ROBERT BRAULT

If things go well with the family,
life is worth living; when the
family falters, life falls apart.

MICHAEL NOVAK

Happiness is not a station you arrive at
but a manner of traveling.

MARGARET LEE RUNBECK

OUR FAMILY

Our family is a circle of love and
strength. With every birth and every
union, the circle grows. Every joy shared
adds more love. Every crisis faced
together makes the circle stronger.

ANONYMOUS